Medieval
World

HEALTH
AND MEDICINE

SAVIOUR PIROTTA

A⁺
Smart Apple Media

First published in the UK by Franklin Watts
96 Leonard Street, London EC2A 4XD

Produced by Arcturus Publishing Ltd.
26/27 Bickels Yard, 151-153 Bermondsey Street, London SE1 3HA
Copyright © 2004 Arcturus Publishing Ltd.

Series concept: Alex Woolf
Editor: Clare Weaver
Designer: Chris Halls, Mind's Eye Design Ltd., Lewes
Illustrator: Adam Hook
Picture researcher: Glass Onion Pictures

Published in the United States by Smart Apple Media
2140 Howard Drive West, North Mankato, MN 56003

Library of Congress Control Number: 2004104273

ISBN 1-58340-573-9

9 8 7 6 5 4 3 2 1

Picture Acknowledgements: AKG Images 5, 19, /British Library 7; The Art
Archive 15, 28, /Biblioteca Nazionale Marciana Venice/Dagli Orti 26, 27, /Museo
della Civilta Romana Rome/Dagli Orti (A) 10, /National Museum Damascus
Syria/Dagli Orti 17, /Palazzo Ducale Urbino/Dagli Orti (A) 4, /Santa Maria della
Scala Hospital Siena, Dagli Orti 18, /Topkapi Museum Istanbul/Dagli Orti 16;
Bridgeman Art Library/Archives Charmet 22, /Bildarchiv Steffens 21, /Giraudon
8, 13, /Lauros/Giraudon 25, /Osterreichische Nationalbibliothek Vienna 23,
/Trustees of the Weston Park Foundation 29; Science and Society Museum Picture
Library 20; Zul Mukhida 9.

CONTENTS

BEFORE THE MIDDLE AGES

The Middle Ages lasted from around A.D. 500 to 1500. Long before this period, ancient Greeks had made huge advances in the understanding of disease and illness. By the fifth century B.C., Greek physicians had started to move away from the idea—still believed by most of the population—that illness and death were caused by magic, or vengeful gods.

The eminent physician and writer Hippocrates (c. 460–377 B.C.) was one of the first to approach medicine as a science. He encouraged doctors to look for natural causes of sickness in their patients, not supernatural ones. He advised them to observe the patient, decide what he or she was suffering from, and then prescribe medicine, usually made from plants.

Hippocrates tried to treat illness by prescribing drugs and changes to diet.

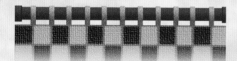

The Hippocratic Oath
Hippocrates was an ancient Greek doctor who became known as the father of medicine and was regarded as the greatest physician of his time. He developed an Oath of Medical Ethics, a code of conduct for practicing physicians, which is still adhered to by doctors today.
"If I fulfill this oath and do not violate it, may it be granted to me to enjoy life and art, being honored with fame among all men for all time to come; if I transgress it and swear falsely, may the opposite of all this be my lot."
(From the *Hippocratic Oath*, c. 400 B.C.)

The ancient Romans, whose understanding of medicine was largely based on that of the Greeks, put great emphasis on public health. Their main cities had a constant supply of fresh water, public baths, hospitals, gymnasiums, and sewage systems. Rome itself, in the early A.D. 300s, had a population of 1.5 million, and boasted 1,352 drinking fountains, 967 bathhouses, and 144 public lavatories.

With the collapse of the Roman empire in A.D. 476, the Romans' achievements in public health and sanitation were lost. As Christianity spread through the former empire, the focus shifted from physical matters to spiritual ones. People concentrated on keeping their soul healthy, not their earthly body. Taking an interest in the body was seen as sinful. Public bathing was discouraged and eventually banned. Death and disease were believed to be the wages of sin. The Church taught its followers that medicine and surgery worked only because God and the saints wanted them to. Without prayer and the repentance of sin, cure was not possible.

The Church expected its followers to submit without question to the Christian faith. Study and scholarship were frowned upon, as students might stray from the teachings of the Church into heresy (a belief that contadicts Church doctrine). Clergymen, who were among the few educated people in Europe at that time, were discouraged by the Church from practicing medicine, because of its focus on the body. As a result, progress in medicine came to a virtual standstill in Europe for several hundred years.

It was not until the 13th century, when learned texts from the Muslim world began to arrive in Europe, that new advances in medical understanding were made.

Saints Preserve Us

People in the Middle Ages believed that some saints could bring about miracle cures. Those who suffered from a disorder of the nervous system called chorea would always pray to St. Vitus, an early Christian who was killed by the Romans. In medieval times, this saint became so popular that chorea, or epilepsy, which caused its victims to jerk uncontrollably, became known as St. Vitus' dance. People who suffered from erysipelas, a common disease that affected the skin and made it break out in boils, turned to St. Anthony the Hermit. Soon, the popular term for erysipelas became St. Anthony's fire. When the bubonic plague swept through Europe in the 14th century, people prayed to St. Roch (1295–1397), a monk who was believed to have cured plague victims by making the sign of the cross over their heads.

An 11th-century German engraving showing people in a churchyard, suffering from St. Vitus' dance.

SICKNESS AND DISEASE

Infant Mortality

Physicians in the Middle Ages were fond of saying that they could cure anyone between the ages of 7 and 70. Young children of the time were very prone to infections, due to malnutrition and lack of hygiene in the home. The first year of a child's life was especially difficult, even more so if the mother could not breastfeed. Many women, especially those of noble birth, were required to produce heirs. As the mortality (death) rate was high, they married in their early teens, which gave them more time to have children, some of whom might live into adulthood. In effect, this meant that many mothers were forced to have babies before they were strong enough to do so. Many women perished during childbirth; others produced infants that could not combat infections and disease.

Waste was often poured from people's windows onto the street below.

In the Middle Ages, only 10 to 15 percent of the population inhabited urban areas; the rest lived in the countryside. Sanitation in the towns and cities, as well as in the countryside, was very poor. Most houses did not have plumbing or access to fresh water for bathing and washing.

Indoor toilets were unheard of; people used outside latrines. At night they used chamber pots, and the contents of these were usually disposed of on the street just outside the house, causing germs to spread. This general lack of hygiene led to a host of killer diseases, including typhoid, typhus, cholera, and dysentery.

Typhoid and cholera spread through communities when human excrement entered the public water supply, while typhus was caused by lice in people's hair and clothes. It didn't always kill its victims, but they remained carriers for the rest of their lives, spreading the disease to people they came in contact with.

Poor diet and coarse clothing also caused many skin-related conditions, including scurvy, scabies, and scrofula. Inadequate storage of grain was the cause of a terrible disease, St. Anthony's fire (see page 5), which blistered and deformed its victims before they died. Rancid food was commonly consumed. The bad taste was masked by rich sauces and sweet-smelling herbs, but these did not prevent food poisoning.

Country people did not live in the same cramped conditions as city-dwellers, but they faced health hazards nonetheless. Many lived in wooden hovels with thatched roofs, which harbored all kinds of vermin. The droppings of rats, birds, and other creatures often ended up in the food of those living below.

For those living close to marshy land and stagnant water, there was another deadly hazard: malaria. Between A.D. 900 and 1300, Europe experienced an uncharacteristically warm climate, creating the perfect breeding ground for the mosquito, which carried the disease.

Life for the rich was less fraught with danger. They had access to clean water and bathed regularly, often in heated water to avoid catching pneumonia. The rich could also afford to eat more fresh food and employed cooks trained in the art of preserving fish and meat. If they fell ill, the nobility had access to the best medical care available.

Lepers were often required to ring a bell to warn passers-by of their presence.

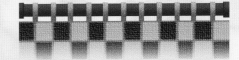

The Leper's Lot

Leprosy, a disease that affects the skin and nerves, was common in the Middle Ages. As it was highly contagious, victims were isolated in communities, either in abandoned villages or in monasteries run by brave monks.

"I forbid you to ever enter a church, a monastery, a fair, a mill, a market, or an assembly of people. I forbid you to leave your house unless dressed in your recognizable garb [clothing] and also shod. I forbid you to wash your hands or to launder anything or to drink at any stream or fountain, unless using your own barrel or dipper. . . . I command you, if accosted by anyone while traveling on a road, to set yourself down-wind of them before you answer. I forbid you to enter any narrow passage, lest a passer-by bump against you."

(From the "Mass of Separation," a 13th-century medieval ritual conducted by a priest to officially separate a leper from his community)

PHYSICIANS, SURGEONS, AND HEALERS

Sick people in the Middle Ages had access to various medical practitioners and healers, depending on their wealth and where they lived. The rich could consult physicians, who were few in number, and mostly based in cities. Physicians trained for five years. Drawn mainly from the ranks of the clergy, their education not only prepared them for practicing medicine but also equipped them to teach their skills to others. Physicians were the wealthiest and highest-ranking members of the medical community. They rarely conducted physical examinations, preferring to diagnose illnesses by questioning patients or analyzing urine samples.

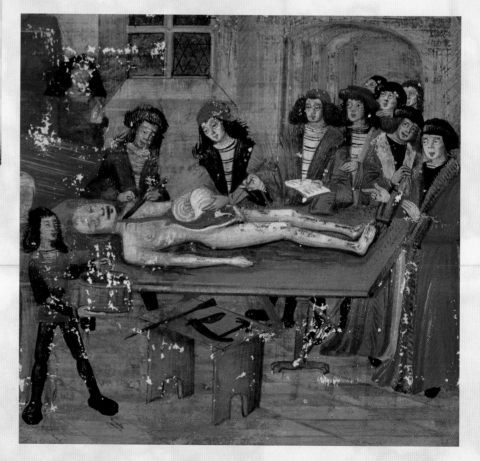

In this 14th-century illustration, a corpse is dissected during an anatomy lesson at the University of Montpellier.

The modern-day barber's pole is a reminder of the previous role of barbers as part-time surgeons.

Surgeons performed most of the operations that physicians considered beneath them, such as setting broken bones and closing wounds. They trained by being apprenticed to other surgeons, and relied more on practical experience than books. They delivered babies by caesarean section, treated hemorrhages, removed gallstones, and carried out bloodlettings (cutting a vein to draw out infected blood).

Barbers carried out operations on poor people who could not afford to see a surgeon. They also pulled teeth and cut people's hair. Barbers stood well below surgeons in the medical hierarchy. However, by the 15th century, their practical knowledge had come to be appreciated, and surgeons reluctantly accepted them as colleagues. Now called barber-surgeons, they had to receive formal training before they could practice. In France, they were required to attend the Faculte de Medicine, where they attended lectures and took an examination.

People who could not afford to see physicians, surgeons, or even barbers could turn to medical practitioners called leeches. Like the barbers, leeches did not have any formal training but performed many of the same duties, although they preferred to use herbal and folk remedies. Some learned their craft by watching and assisting surgeons.

The majority of those living in the countryside had access only to unlicensed herbalists or folk healers. They offered cures ranging from herbs and plants with healing properties to magical charms. Remedies included swallowing spiders encased in raisins to cure ague (fever) and tying bags of buttercups around victims' necks to ward off insanity. Most folk healers were women, and their arts were often passed on from mother to daughter.

The Barber's Sign
Many people wonder why, even today, barbers have a sign outside their shop showing a white staff with a twisting red stripe. The custom started in the Middle Ages, when barbers often performed bloodletting. The pole itself is a reminder of a stick that patients used to hold tightly during the procedure. The pressure expanded the veins, so helping the blood to flow more easily. The white and red stripes represent the bandages and blood.

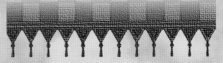

THE FOUR HUMORS

Medieval doctors believed that the dominant humor in a person dictated his temperament. People were prone to have more of one fluid in their bodies than any of the other three. Those who had more blood than the other three fluids were "sanguine," meaning happy and generous. Those who had too much yellow bile were labeled "choleric." They would behave violently and were in a permanently vengeful mood. Patients with too much phlegm were "phlegmatic," and tended to be pale and cowardly. Gluttonous, lazy, and sentimental behavior was seen as a sign of excess black bile. A person with this condition was called "melancholic."

Throughout the Middle Ages, medical techniques were based on theories developed by the ancient Greeks. Hippocrates (c. 470–377 B.C.) taught that people had four kinds of liquids in their bodies, known as humors. These were blood, yellow bile, black bile and phlegm. They gave off vapors, which affected a person's mood and health.

Galen (A.D. 130–201) also believed in the theory of the four humors. He insisted that a person's health depended on an equal balance of the four humors in their bodies; an imbalance was the cause of most sicknesses and diseases. People could maintain the correct balance of humors in their body by following the right diet or by taking prescribed medicines. The balance of humors was also affected by a person's age, the seasons, and the weather.

Claudius Galen was the first person to make an in-depth study of anatomy.

Galen's teaching influenced medical thinking for most of the Middle Ages. Doctors did not yet know that blood circulated around the body; they believed that once blood was used it remained stagnant within the body, making possible a build-up of excess blood in the system. They saw fevers, headaches, and, in extreme cases, strokes as symptoms of excess blood.

To restore the balance of humors in a patient, surgeons would often prescribe bloodletting, a process that drew the excess blood out of the body. The amount needed to be drawn was determined by a complex system devised by Galen. It took many factors into consideration, including the time of year, and the age, and sometimes the star sign, of the patient.

Minor bloodletting was done using leeches—large, worm-like creatures that bite through skin and suck blood. The surgeon would apply them to the required spot and then cover them with a glass cup to catch the blood.

If a larger amount of blood needed to be drawn, the surgeon would open a vein with a sharp knife. Blood would be allowed to flow out into a shallow bowl. Sometimes up to four pints (1.9 l) would be removed from a patient in one session. If this caused the patient to faint, it was seen as the first step on the road to recovery.

Bloodletting was used to reduce excess circulation of blood, believed to be a cause of inflammation.

A Choleric Man

Galen describes the qualities of a choleric man:

"We call that man choleric in whose body heat and dryness abound. Such persons are usually short of stature, and not fat, their skin rough and hot in feeling, and their bodies very hairy; the hair of their heads is yellowish, red, or flaxen; the color of their face is tawny or sunburned; they have beards; they have little hollow hazel eyes. . . . their digestion is very strong; their pulse is swift and strong, their urine yellow and thin; they dream of fighting and quarreling."
(From *Art of Physic*, Claudius Galen, c. 207)

HAVING SURGERY

How to Heal a Cracked Skull
"If the wound is narrow, enlarge it, and unless prevented by bleeding, immediately trephine [make holes in the skull] with an iron instrument, very cautiously on both sides of the fissure. Make as many holes as seems wise, then cut the cranium from one whole to another with a bistoury [scalpel], so that the incision extends to the edge of the fissure. Carefully remove pus oozing from above the cerebrum [brain] with a silk from a fine linen cloth introduced sideways between the cerebrum and cranium by means of a feather. . . ."
(From *Chirurgia*, c. 1300, by the Italian surgeon Roland of Parma)

A surgeon places a patient's leg in a splint. The most frequent demand for medical help was for the treatment of injuries.

Surgery in the Middle Ages was fraught with danger. Many patients remained awake during operations. The majority died of shock or pain before the surgery was finished. There were no antiseptics, and those who survived the ordeal often succumbed to infection afterwards.

Surgery was therefore usually performed only as a last resort, when all other treatments had failed. The most common operations were minor ones. Surgeons removed cataracts from eyes, reset broken bones, adjusted dislocated bones, and repaired hernias.

Surgeons often used plants and herbs for pain relief. These included mandragora, the root of the poisonous mandrake

plant. Cannabis, opium, and a poisonous herb called deadly nightshade were also used. Some surgeons used alcohol, or a mixture of mandrake and wine.

The anesthetics were administered by inhalation or drinking. Sometimes a sea sponge, called the *spongia somnifera*, was dipped in wine and held under the patient's nose until he or she passed out. It was difficult for surgeons to gauge the right amount of drug needed for a particular patient. Some would continually tweak a patient's nose during the operation to make sure he or she had not died. Hugh of Lucca, an Italian doctor who practiced in the early 13th century, would tie his patients to the operating table in case the patient woke up halfway through the surgery.

Les Pierres de la Folie
Many fake doctors operated throughout the Middle Ages. Some even specialized in brain surgery! Barber-surgeons traveled from town to town, offering to cure madness. They would cut into a patient's skull in a bid to remove stones that were believed to grow in the brain and cause insanity. Of course, these "stones of madness," or "Pierres de la folie," as they were known, did not exist.

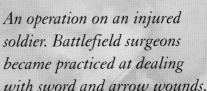

An operation on an injured soldier. Battlefield surgeons became practiced at dealing with sword and arrow wounds.

Surgeons also treated injured soldiers on battlefields. They dug bullets out of wounds, sealed torn flesh, and amputated limbs where gangrene had set in. Gunpowder wounds were believed to be poisonous, just like snake bites. Surgeons would cauterize the wounds by pouring boiling oil into them. They also sealed wounds by applying red-hot pokers to the open flesh. The process burned the skin so that not enough of it was left to cover over the amputation. As a result, many soldiers either bled to death or died from infection.

GOING TO THE DENTIST

Albucasis of Cordoba

Albucasis, a Muslim surgeon, was a pioneer in the treatment of teeth. His methods are influential to this day, and several modern dental instruments are based on designs illustrated in his books. These included files for removing decay, forceps for extracting teeth, and scrapers. Albucasis identified tartar as a danger to gums, and recommended regular scaling to remove this. He also encouraged his patients to polish their teeth with fine abrasives until they were white. Albucasis believed teeth should be extracted only as a last resort, and he condemned barbers who carried out this practice without proper care.

Qualified dentists were called "dentatores." They were trained at a university and were extremely expensive, so few people could afford their services. Dentatores believed that tooth decay was caused by tiny worms in the mouth. They used scrapers to remove rotten parts of teeth, and filled cavities with metal fillings, sometimes made of gold. Loose teeth were strengthened with metal bindings. Their array of implements included saws, forceps, and files.

Barber-surgeons were also licensed to pull teeth, and unqualified tooth-drawers were available at fairs and markets all over Europe. They usually wore necklaces strung with teeth to show how many people had trusted them with extractions. They prided themselves on their ability to pull out teeth with as little pain as possible.

Between 700 and 1200, Muslim Arabs made great advances in oral science. They discovered ways to straighten crooked teeth and make false molars from animal bones. This knowledge gradually filtered through to the dentatores of Europe.

As tooth-drawers did their work, an assistant would play a drum to drown out the customer's cries of pain.

A collection of dental instruments illustrated in Albucasis' famous 14th-century medical encyclopedia.

While European barber-surgeons and tooth-drawers concentrated on pulling teeth, enlightened Arab physicians advocated it only if no other option was available. The renowned surgeon Albucasis of Cordoba, who lived from 1013 to 1106, believed that everything should be done to save a broken tooth. In his writings he gave detailed information on how to bind and repair broken teeth.

Albucasis pioneered many new methods of dentistry, including splinting and bridging teeth. He also advised his patients to clean their teeth with an early form of tooth powder, realizing that oral hygiene kept the gums healthy. His work greatly influenced European dentistry.

In France, a physician named Guy de Chauliac (1300–68) also promoted the importance of oral hygiene in his writings. De Chauliac was the first doctor to refer to dentatores in his work, writing that they were not mere teeth-pullers but qualified professionals who also treated infected tissue in the mouth. In the early 1400s, another dental pioneer, Giovanni de Arcoli, urged people to avoid hot, cold, or sweet foods and was the first to mention the use of gold fillings.

People who could not afford to visit a dentatore, a barber-surgeon, or even a tooth-drawer at the market could see a folk healer. She would let them touch a tooth taken from a dead person. The ritual was supposed to cure their ailment.

Dental Advice
Guy de Chauliac gave the following tips to his patients: "First, no perishables such as fish or dairy products should be taken.
Second, excessively hot or cold food should be avoided, especially one immediately following the other.
Third, no hard things should be chewed, such as bones.
Fourth, foods known to be harmful to teeth, such as leeks, should be avoided.
Fifth, the teeth should not be picked in a painful or rough manner.
Sixth, they should be rubbed with honey and burned salt."
(From *Chirurgia Magna*, 1363, Guy de Chauliac)

MEDICAL TEXTBOOKS

Although the Christian Church frowned on medical study, it was the monasteries who kept the teachings of the Greeks and Romans alive. As the only people with the knowledge to translate the ancient manuscripts into Latin, monks became the guardians of these texts, copying them down and making them available for physicians.

As a Roman army surgeon, Dioscorides (on the right) was able to travel extensively, and he discovered medicinal plants in many different parts of the empire.

Epilepsy
Avicenna describes epilepsy in his *Canon of Medicine*: "Epilepsy is a disease which prevents the organs affected from using the senses, moving, and walking upright. It is caused by a blockage. Usually there is a general seizure, caused by some damage, which affects the front cerebral ventricle, making it impossible for the person affected to remain standing upright."
(From *Canon of Medicine*, 11th century, by Avicenna)

It was through the work of the monasteries that medical students had access to the teachings of Hippocrates and Galen. They also studied the works of many other authors, including *De Materia Medica*, written by a Greek army doctor named Pedanius Dioscorides in the first century A.D. A surgeon employed by the Roman army, Dioscorides wrote his five-volume work based on experience gained during his travels.

The books listed about 1,000 simple medicines, mostly natural remedies derived from plants and animal products such as milk and honey, but also chemicals such as mercury and lead acetate. Dioscorides' work remained the basis for the study of pharmacology until the end of the 15th century.

One of the most comprehensive medical texts of the Middle Ages, dating from around 1230, was the *Compendium of Medicine*, written by Gilbertus Anglicus. His work offers detailed advice on the treatment of wounds, especially those caused by arrows. It is the first medical text to mention the use of splints and plaster casts for broken joints. The *Compendium* covers treatment for all parts of the human body, including the head, eyes, ears, nose, mouth, and teeth. The book had a major impact on the medieval world, and Gilbertus is even mentioned by Geoffrey Chaucer in his poem *The Canterbury Tales*.

In the 12th century, western Europeans discovered the works of an Iranian scholar named Avicenna, or Ibn Sina (980–1037). His books included *Kitab ash-shifa* (*Book of Healing*), a philosophical and scientific encyclopedia, and the *Canon of Medicine*, which was based on the work of ancient Greek physicians, such as Galen, as well as his own scholarship. After its translation into Latin, the *Canon* remained the undisputed medical authority in Europe for hundreds of years. Medieval physicians accorded Avicenna the same respect as Galen and Hippocrates.

Pliny the Elder

The prolific Roman author Pliny the Elder (A.D. 23–79) wrote the *Historia Naturali*, or *Natural History*. This exhaustive encyclopedia of 37 volumes encompasses the science, history, and geography of the world. Some of the volumes describe common diseases and conditions of the time, including leprosy, lack of sexual appetite, dandruff, and toothache. The author also discusses medicines made from wild plants, garden produce, trees, and the bones of wild animals such as elephants and lions.

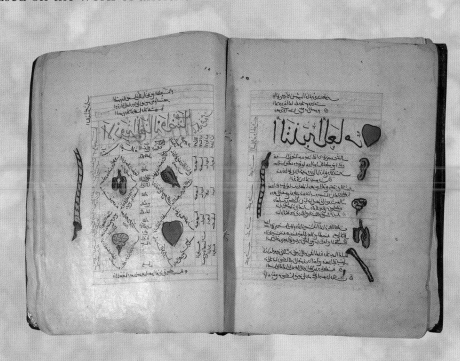

Pages from Avicenna's Canon of Medicine.

MONASTERIES AND HOSPITALS

Knights and Monks

By the time the first Crusade reached Jerusalem in 1099, there were already several hospitals there, built mainly to look after pilgrims visiting the Holy Land. One of these hospitals was established by a rich merchant from Amalfi, Italy, named Mauro. After the conquest of the city by the crusaders, the monk running this hospital was given permission to build a new one near the church of Saint John the Baptist. From this grew the Order of the Knights of Saint John, an organization of knights who were also monks. They built more hospitals, not only in Jerusalem but also in many European cities along the pilgrim route to the Holy Land. Several were built in ports where pilgrims waited for ships.

Santa Maria della Scala Hospital in Siena.

Following the example of Christ, the early Christians considered it their duty to care for and try to heal the sick. By the fourth century A.D., special buildings to house the ill were being built. In 375, a monk named St. Ephraem provided 300 beds for sufferers of the plague at Edessa. In 369, St. Basil founded a hospital in Caesarea, Cappadocia (in present-day Turkey). It was the size of a small town, with streets, quarters for nurses and physicians, different halls separating patients according to their disease, and workshops where tools and bandages could be made.

By the 10th century, most monasteries in Europe had a hospital attached to them, where monks would care for sick people. The example was set by the Benedictine abbey of

Cluny in France, founded in 910. Cluny was the first to have a "hospitale pauperum," which was an infirmary for the poor. Between the 11th and 16th centuries, the Roman Catholic Church funded and built some 750 hospitals in England alone. In 13th-century Paris, there were at least 12 hospitals, all funded by the Church. They were run by monks and staffed by nuns and lay Christians.

The Knights of St. John preparing for battle in 1480. They were also well-known for founding and maintaining hospitals for pilgrims.

Grand Hospital of Milan
A 19th-century American, Dr. W. Gill Wylie, describes a visit to a medieval Italian hospital:
"In 1456 the Grand Hospital of Milan was opened. This remarkable building is still in use as a hospital and contains usually more than 2,000 patients. . . . The main wards . . . form a cross, in the center of which is a cupola [dome], with an altar beneath it, where divine service is performed daily in sight of the patients. These wards have corridors on both sides, which are not so lofty as the ceilings of the wards, and consequently there is plenty of room for windows above these passages. The ceilings are 30 or 40 feet [9–12 m] high, and the floors covered with red bricks or flags. The outside wards are nothing but spacious corridors."
(From an 1876 essay)

Most hospitals were built in the cities, within easy reach of the poor. Where possible they were located near rivers, where the air was cleaner. Some hospitals, such as the famous Santa Maria Nuova in Florence, were built outside city walls, where it was easier to control the spread of contagious diseases.

No one was ever turned away from a hospital. Muslims and Jews, as well as Christians, were admitted, as were the homeless, the elderly, and pilgrims from foreign countries. On arrival, patients were bathed and treated for lice, and their clothes were washed. Most were given their own beds, though during busy periods they had to share with others. While in the hospital they were expected to pray for their fellow patients and the benefactors who built and maintained the establishment.

Towards the end of the Middle Ages, city authorities became more involved in the funding and administering of hospitals. However, monks and nuns continued to play an important role in tending the sick.

WOMEN IN MEDIEVAL MEDICINE

During the Middle Ages, a great many women were involved in the provision of healthcare and medicine, not just as folk healers, but also as nurses and midwives. Nurses worked mainly in hospitals. Their primary duties involved washing, dressing, and feeding the ill. They were also expected to wash soiled linen and prepare the dead for burial. Most nurses joined a monastic order, dedicating their entire lives to the curing of the sick. Rich people would sometimes hire a nurse to look after a patient at home.

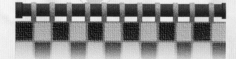

A midwife attends a woman in labor.

Midwives learned their trade by assisting more experienced practitioners. They mixed practical knowledge with superstitious practices inherited from their elders. A good midwife, for example, would have the foresight to use pepper to cause violent sneezing, thus inducing birth. But she might also open all the drawers, doors, and bottles in the room to make sure no evil spirits were hiding there during the mother's labor.

Midwives

A Spanish lawyer, Domingo de Cuerla, oversees the work of the midwife Catalina in 1490, in Zaragoza:
"And thus, having seen and examined the baby myself, and he being a man as has been said, the aforementioned Catalina, midwife, before me, the notary [lawyer], and the witnesses mentioned below, cut the umbilical cord of the aforesaid child and wrapped him in a cloth."
(From the public record of the labor of Isabel de la Cavalleria, 1490)

Before midwives could practice, they had to obtain a document from their local parish priest attesting to their good character. A document from 1490, written by a lawyer from Cordoba, details the birth of a nobleman's child. He describes how he searched the two midwives present at the birth to make sure that they had not smuggled another infant into the room under their skirts. He also states that they both took oaths, which bound them to deliver the baby safely and "without fraud."

In 1221, the Holy Roman Emperor Fredrick II decreed that no one could practice medicine without a university qualification. This effectively barred women from the profession, as they were forbidden to attend universities.

In 1322, the medical faculty of Paris prosecuted Jacqueline Felicie de Almania for operating without a license. During her trial she argued that women doctors should be allowed to treat female patients. It was impossible for men to examine them properly, as male doctors could only attend to female patients covered by a blanket. The court ignored her plea and banned her from practicing.

Some wealthy women did manage to attend medical schools. Of these, the most famous was Trotula, who lived in the early 13th century. She was the leader of a group called "the ladies of Salerno." An experienced midwife, she wrote at length about gynecology, obstetrics, birth control, and infertility. Her most influential work was *Passionibus Mulierum Curandorum* (*The Diseases of Women*).

Hildegard of Bingen

Hildegard of Bingen was a German abbess who lived from 1098 to 1179. An educated woman of noble birth, she wrote many books, including *Physica* and *Causae et Curae* (*Causes and Cures*). They were both works about the healing powers of natural objects. Her medical ideas were based on the classical philosophy first expounded by Hippocrates. The abbess also believed in the healing power of music, and composed many works that are still played today.

Hildegard of Bingen. Her medical books remained influential long after her death.

THE USE OF HERBAL MEDICINES

The doctors of ancient Rome collected a vast amount of knowledge, inherited from the Greeks and the Egyptians, on the uses and medicinal properties of herbs, plants, flowers, and fruit. Medieval monks benefited from this ancient wisdom by translating the Roman texts and by applying what they learned in their own infirmaries and hospitals.

Monks gather plants and prepare medicines. Herbal remedies were often used to restore a humor imbalance.

The Power of Color
The physician-gardener Paracelsus (1493–1541) believed that every herb had its own "sign." The shape, scent, and color of a plant, as well as the environment it flourished in, told a healer what its properties were. According to Paraclesus, marigolds and dandelions could cure jaundice, a disease that made a patient's skin look yellow; pansies, with their heart-shaped petals, could be used for heart trouble.

All monasteries kept a special garden where the monks grew medicinal herbs to help the sick. Making and administering herbal medicines required no formal training. In order to produce a potion, a monk or folk healer needed only to be able to read.

Monks and herbalists believed that all diseases could be cured with herbs, plants, and spices. Parsley, for example, was used to help cure water retention, as well as epilepsy. Indeed, some herbs were regarded as a tonic against a whole host of maladies and illnesses. Anise, an herb of the carrot family, was prescribed to combat mucus in the respiratory system, freshen the breath, help the digestion, stop hiccups, banish lice from children's hair, and deal with infant colic. It was also seen as a powerful cure for asthma, insomnia, nausea, and headaches.

Blackberries were prescribed as a cure for gout; in fact, they were often known as "goutberries." People also chewed the leaves and bark of the blackberry tree to stop gums from bleeding, while a syrup of the same fruit was eaten as a treatment for dysentery.

Some herbs were not only used as medicines, but were also seen to possess the power of charms. For example, wild celery, also known as angelica, was used by herbalists as a cough remedy, but people also made necklaces from it to ward off evil and sickness. It was said that witches never touched the plant, as its healing properties could destroy their powers. During the witch hunts of the late Middle Ages, many women were saved from burning when the medicinal plant was found in their cupboards.

The practitioners of herbal medicine often tried to add an air of mystery to their art by combining it with incantations and prayers to the saints. However, with the invention of printing in the 15th century, herbalist manuals became more widely available, and the practice was demystified.

In this 14th-century painting, a mother and daughter gather dill, a medicinal herb used to treat eye diseases and stomach-ache. It was also believed to protect people from witchcraft.

A Remedy for Ailments of the Lungs
Many illnesses called for potions made out of several herbs. The famous herbalist Gilbertus Anglicus recommended a special syrup for curing lung conditions: "Take barley water which has been strained, raisins, violets, jujube, seed of melon and gourd, wheat starch, licorice, black plums, fennel root, parsley, wild celery, anise, caraway, and make thereof a syrup. That is to say, seep all these in water until the virtue of them be in the water. Then strain it and add sugar or honey. And then set it over the fire to steep softly. Then take the white of four eggs and beat them well and add them. And always skim it until it is clear. Then take it down and strain it clean so that no dregs remain therein. Put it in a closed vessel."
(From *Compendium of Medicine*, started in 1230, Gilbertus Anglicus)

THE HEALING PILGRIMAGE

A Nun's Pilgrimage
Between A.D. 381 and 384, a Spanish nun named Egeria went on a pilgrimage to the Holy Land. In a letter to the sisters in her convent, she described Mount Sinai: "So at ten o'clock we arrived on the summit of Sinai. . . . The church which is now there is not impressive for its size (there is too little room on the summit), but it has a grace all its own. And when with God's help we had climbed right to the top and reached the door of this church, there was the presbyter, the one who is appointed to the church, coming to meet us from his cell. He was a healthy old man, a monk from his boyhood and an 'ascetic' as they call it here—in fact just the man for the place."

A pilgrim at Canterbury kneels before a casket depicting the murder of Thomas Becket.

Throughout the Middle Ages, the Church encouraged people to make pilgrimages to special holy places where saints were buried. Those who made these journeys believed that if they prayed at these shrines, the saints could perform miracles, including making sick people well again.

As early as the fourth century A.D., people traveled from Bordeaux to Jerusalem to be cured at the places where Jesus had lived. However, pilgrimages reached a peak of popularity between the 11th and 14th centuries.

Sin was believed to be the root cause of illness, and pilgrims gladly endured the hardships of their journeys as penance for their sinful lives. On reaching their destination, pilgrims could pray to the saints at the places where they had lived and performed miracles. They could touch relics or objects that the holy ones had used in their lives.

The most popular shrine in England was the tomb of Thomas Becket at Canterbury. As Archbishop, Becket was murdered for his faith on December 29, 1170. Word soon spread that his followers had managed to dip pieces of cloth in his blood. Anyone who touched these, it was believed, would be cured of blindness and leprosy. At the cathedral, the sick could touch the rags and buy bottles of Becket's blood.

The second most popular British shrine could be visited in Walsingham. In 1061, a Saxon noblewoman named Richeldis de Faverches had a vision in which she was told to construct a replica of the house where the Virgin Mary had lived. She did so, and the building became known as the Shrine of Our Lady of Walsingham. People flocked there to pray in front of a sealed glass jar that was said to contain the milk of the Virgin Mary. A spring nearby was believed to cure pains in the head and stomach.

However, the most venerated shrine of medieval times was the Cathedral of Santiago de Compostela in Spain. Believed to be the place where the body of Saint James, one of the apostles, was buried, it became one of the most visited sites in Europe during the 12th and 13th centuries. Visitors to the great cathedral there claimed to have been cured of many illnesses.

Royal Pilgrimage
People of all classes undertook pilgrimages, even royalty. Many of the kings and queens of England journeyed to Walsingham, including Henry VIII, who walked the last mile in bare feet. He went there to pray for a son. In 1538, Henry outlawed all abbeys in England. The monastery at Walsingham was reduced to rubble, and a mansion was built in its place. On the king's orders the statue of the Madonna was burned to cinders. The shrine of Walsingham, known in the Middle Ages as Britain's Nazareth, was not restored until the 20th century.

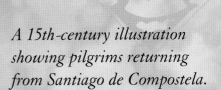

A 15th-century illustration showing pilgrims returning from Santiago de Compostela.

THE BLACK DEATH

The Flagellants

Many regarded the plague as a punishment from God. They believed that doing penance in public would prevent them from getting the disease. Bands of people took to the streets, singing hymns and praying. They were called flagellants because they flagellated (whipped) themselves in public. The flagellants attacked any Jews they came across on their wanderings, accusing them of crucifying Christ and helping to invite the plague into Europe. In 1349, Pope Clement VI denounced them and ordered the authorities to stop them from wandering around towns and villages. The flagellants were not to be deterred, and hordes of them would gather every time an outbreak of the Black Death occurred.

The bodies of plague victims who died overnight were laid in the street, ready to be carted away for burial.

In October 1347, 12 Genoese galley ships sailed into the harbor at Messina, in Sicily, full of dying men. The sailors were suffering from a mysterious and terrifying disease that had turned their skin a dark purple, and swelled their tongues and their arms. The authorities ordered the ships to leave the harbor, but it was too late: people had already come into contact with the sailors. The disease spread to the city, and its fleeing inhabitants carried the disease to the rest of Sicily. The plague, known as the Black Death, had arrived in Europe.

The plague was a disease that first affected fleas, and was then passed on to rats. The rats acted as carriers, spreading death through the dirty towns and cities. The disease reached Italy, Spain, England, and France in 1348, and the following year it spread to Austria, Holland, Hungary, Switzerland, and Germany. By 1350, the Black Death had reached Scandinavia and the Baltic countries.

The doctors of Europe, with no previous knowledge of the disease, tried in vain to cure it. Victims were told to wash their bodies with vinegar and water, and to stay in bed. The swellings were cut open in the hope that the disease would flow out. Poultices made from tree resin and lily roots were applied to the cuts. Some surgeons tried bloodletting.

Special plague medicines went on sale. One was made of ground eggshells, chopped marigold petals, and treacle boiled in ale, to be taken twice a day. Folk healers recommended drinking urine and holding a live hen against the swellings in a bid to draw the disease into the bird. Nothing worked. The majority of victims died within three days.

Whole towns and villages were wiped out. In the cities, normal life came to a stop. Authority vanished as priests, judges, and community leaders died or fled. Criminals were released from jail, as there was no one left to guard them. The dead were buried in great pits by farmers and former prisoners.

Between 1348 and 1351, 25 million people died of the plague in Europe, one-fourth of the population. In despair, many turned to God for help. Women whose husbands had died became nuns. Flagellants did penance on the streets (see panel on page 26). By 1400, there had been five more outbreaks of the disease, and the plague was to remain a recurrent fear until the 17th century.

The Writer's View
Bocaccio, an Italian author who was born in 1313, wrote about the plague and its effects on Europe in his book *The Decameron*. Here is a vivid scene he described: "The rags of a poor man who had just died from the disease were thrown into the public street and were noticed by two pigs, who, following their custom, pressed their snouts into the rags, and afterwards picked them up with their teeth, and shook them against their cheeks: and within a short time, they both began to convulse, and they both, the two of them, fell dead on the ground next to the evil rags."
(From *The Decameron*, 1350, by Bocaccio)

Flagellants walked two-by-two in long columns of up to 300.

TOWARDS THE 16TH CENTURY

An Accidental Discovery

The French surgeon Paré describes in his journal his chance discovery of a new, humane form of disinfection: "At last I wanted oil, and was constrained instead to apply a digestive of yolks of eggs, oil of roses, and turpentine. In the night I could not sleep in quiet, fearing some default in not cauterizing, that I should those to whom I had not used the burning oil dead impoisoned; which made me rise very early to visit them, where beyond my expectation I found those whom I had applied my digestive medicine, to feel little pain, and their wound without inflammation or tumor, having rested reasonable well in the night: the others to whom was used the said boiling oil, I found them feverish, with great pain. . . . And then I resolved with myself never to so cruelly burn poor men wounded with gunshot."
(From *Journeys in Diverse Places*, 1580, Ambroise Paré)

The plague had a major effect on medieval society. The Church was damaged by the loss of so many of its clergy. It had also been made to seem powerless by its failure to save the lives of the faithful. Another effect of the plague was to promote further studies in medicine. It was clear that traditional medical teaching could provide no answer to this new disease, and this encouraged scholars to look more closely at how the human body actually worked, rather than relying on ancient theories.

For most of the Middle Ages, the Church forbade the dissection of human corpses because of the Christian belief in the resurrection of the body. Therefore all anatomical study had to be performed on animals. However, in the 15th century, surgeons began cutting up human bodies for study.

Ambroise Paré performing an operation near a battlefield.

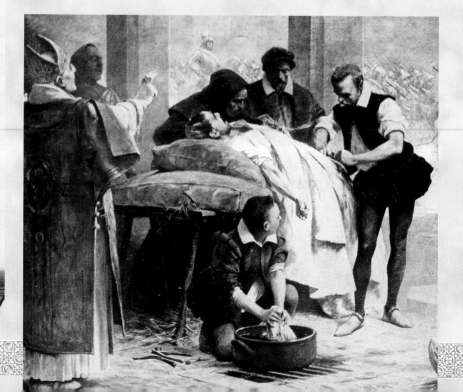

William Harvey (1578–1657), who discovered how blood was pumped by the heart around the body.

In 1543, a young Belgian physician named Andreas Vesalius published a book entitled *De Humani Corpris Fabrica* (*On the Structure of the Human Body*). It was based on observations carried out during dissections. The book corrected many of the errors made by Galen, whose work had heavily influenced medieval understanding of anatomy.

Vesalius' work was continued by the Italian anatomist Hieronymus Fabricius. Born in 1537, Fabricius was the first to publish detailed studies of the placenta and the human embryo. He also discovered that the pupil of the eye changes its size. But his most important work was the discovery of folds, or valves, inside human veins.

The new study of anatomy also had a positive effect on surgical techniques. The French surgeon Ambroise Paré (1510–90) discovered a way of disinfecting and stopping wounds that also minimized suffering. While attending to wounded soldiers on a battlefield, Paré ran out of oil, which was used to literally fry wounds shut. Instead, he was forced to use a mixture of eggs, oil of roses, and turpentine, and this was a great success, earning him the title of "father of modern surgery."

Medicine made great advances during the 15th and 16th centuries. The idea that illness and death were the wages of sin had been swept aside in many places, to be replaced by a more rational and scientific approach, laying the foundations of modern medicine.

A Germ Theory
In 1546, the Italian doctor Girolamo Fracas Toro put forward the theory that epidemic diseases could be transmitted over long distances by invisible carriers, or germs. He believed that germs could be transferred from one person to another merely by the carriers coming into brief contact. His work preceded that of Louis Pasteur by some 300 years.

TIMELINE

369	St. Basil founds a hospital in Caesarea.
375	St. Ephraem provides 300 beds for plague victims in Edessa.
410	Visigoths conquer Rome.
793	King Offa builds a monastery in St. Albans, which becomes one of the most popular healing shrines of the Middle Ages.
898	Death of Soror, founder of the first monastic order to look after the ill, in Siena, Italy.
910	Founding of the Benedictine abbey in Cluny, France; the first abbey to offer medical treatment to the poor.
924–56	Bald writes the *Leech Book of Bald*.
980	Birth of Muslim scholar Avicenna, who wrote the *Book of Healing* and the *Canon of Medicine*.
1013	Birth of Albucasis, perhaps the greatest surgeon of the Middle Ages.
1061	Richeldis de Faverches founds a holy shrine and a popular destination for pilgrims, at Walsingham, England.
1098	Birth of Hildegard Von Bingen, abbess and influential author of *Causes and Cures*.
1099	The first Crusade reaches Jerusalem.
1170	Thomas Becket is murdered. Canterbury Cathedral becomes the site of alleged miracle healings.
1221	Emperor Fredrick II decrees that no doctor can operate unless he qualifies at the University of Salerno.
c. 1230	Gilbertus Anglicus writes the *Compendium of Medicine*.
1235	Human dissections are allowed at the University of Salerno.
1322	The French courts prosecute Dr. Jacqueline Felicie de Almania for practicing without a license.
1347	Genoese sailors bring the plague to Sicily and Italy.
1348	The plague reaches England.
1351	The plague reaches Russia.
1456	Opening of the Grand Hospital in Milan.
1510	Birth of Ambroise Paré, who pioneered an early method of disinfecting wounds.
1538	Henry VIII closes down many abbeys in England, along with their hospitals.

GLOSSARY AND FURTHER INFORMATION

abbess The leader of a nun's community.

ague A fever that produces swelling at regular intervals.

amputation The cutting of a limb from a body.

amulets Lucky charms.

anesthetic A pain-relieving potion that can cause patients to fall unconscious.

apothecary A pharmacy.

bubonic A type of plague that causes a swelling of the glands, especially those in the groin.

caesarean section Cutting into the womb to deliver a baby.

cataracts A clouding of the eyes that prevents victims from seeing properly.

cathedral The main church of a city.

cauterize Burn shut, especially a wound.

chancellor The head of a university.

cholera A severe disease that affects the intestines and causes diarrhea. It often leads to death.

chorea A sickness of the nerves that makes people shake uncontrollably.

code of conduct A set of rules.

contagious Easily transmitted from one person to another.

dysentery A disease of the lower intestine, caused by infection with bacteria, that gives victims severe diarrhea.

elite A privileged few; the most high-ranking people in a society.

eminent Well-known.

epilepsy A nervous condition that can cause sudden losses of consciousness, often accompanied by convulsions.

erysipelas An acute fever that inflames the skin.

extraction The process of pulling something out, such as teeth.

gallstones Tiny stones that form in people's gallbladders.

gangrene The rotting of parts of the human body.

Genoese From Genoa, a port in Italy.

gout A disease that swells up the joints, usually caused by too much rich food.

hemorrhage Severe bleeding.

herbalist Someone who uses herbs for medicine.

hermit A holy person who shuts himself off from the rest of the world.

hygiene Cleanliness.

infirmary A place for sick people.

insomnia A condition that prevents victims from sleeping.

Latin The language of ancient Rome, used throughout Europe during the Middle Ages as the language of scholarship, government, law, and the Church.

leprosy A disease of the skin and nerves. The skin of its victims becomes scarred and blistered, and their fingers, toes, and parts of their face slowly rot away.

malnutrition Suffering from a lack of food.

monk A man who joins a community of holy people.

mortality rate The rate at which people die within a particular group.

oil of roses A mixture of oil and crushed roses.

paralysis Complete loss of movement in the body.

pilgrimage A journey to a holy site or shrine.

pneumonia A disease that affects the lungs, caused by infection.

pneumonic Relating to the lungs.

poultice A warm, moist preparation applied to a wound.

prolific Highly productive.

rancid Gone sour or rank.

repentance A feeling of regret at having done something wrong.

sanitation Cleanliness.

scabies A contagious skin disease which causes intense itching and inflammation.

scrofula A disease of the glands that causes victims' necks to swell.

scurvy A disease caused by lack of vitamin C. Sufferers often lose their teeth.

shrine A place associated with a holy person or saint.

sign of the cross A gesture made by some Christians before they start praying.

splinting Tying to a splint or support.

surgery Medical treatment that involves cutting open the body.

symptoms Signs of illness.

theology The study of religion and faith.

typhoid A serious, sometimes fatal, infection of the digestive system.

typhus A disease caused by lice, causing fever and rashes.

vapors Gases.

venerated Adored, respected, prayed to.

RECOMMENDED READING

Corzine, Phyllis. *Black Death*. San Diego, Calif.: Lucent Books, 1997.

De Hahn, Tracee. *Black Death*. Philadelphia, Pa.: Chelsea House Publishers, 2001.

Langley, Andrew. *Medieval Life*. New York: DK Publishing, 2000.

Quigley, Mary. *Middle Ages*. Chicago: Heinemann Library, 2002.

RECOMMENDED WEB SITES

http://www.learner.org/exhibits/middleages/health.html

http://history.boisestate.edu/westciv/plague/

http://www.history-magazine.com/black.html

INDEX